Now you see it –
now you don't

René Magritte

Prestel

This house in Brussels, the capital of Belgium, was the home of René Magritte and his wife Georgette for over 20 years, from 1930 to 1954.

René enjoyed reading detective and mystery stories and loved the cinema. Most of all he liked thrillers and comedies with Laurel & Hardy or Charlie Chaplin. Sometimes, for his own entertainment, he actually made some very funny films himself in which he appeared along with Georgette and their friends in unusual and imaginative disguises.

René Magritte was a painter. Behind the curtained windows in this house he sat in front of his easel and painted pictures which are disquieting and mysterious, full of surprises and often unfathomable.

For René Magritte, the whole world was full of mysteries and puzzles. He was interested in what was hiding behind things. Here, for example, when looking at an egg, he already sees the mature bird that, at some point, will hatch out of it.

Why are Magritte's paintings so mysterious?

Magritte used to have a very inquisitive way at looking at simple, everyday objects which everyone knows very well. In his pictures he then transformed them into peculiar apparitions.

Are they really just normal things?

All of a sudden, a comb, a glass, a piece of soap, a shaving brush and a match become enormous – way too big to be usable – and are shown in a bedroom that has walls decorated with a glorious cloudy sky instead of wallpaper. As a result, all of these ordinary objects appear new and exciting – objects which nobody otherwise would pay attention to because they are completely normal.

All the objects shown on the left are hidden in the pictures somewhere in this book. Can you find them?

René Magritte did not recount stories in his paintings like writers
or poets who express themselves in words. As a painter, Magritte could
make his thoughts visible in pictures.

What a horrible meal!

This slice of ham has an eye in the middle. And it's staring right up at us and seems to be watching. Who wouldn't lose their appetite?! The painter gave this work the title *The Portrait*. A portrait is actually a picture of a person, usually painted so that you can see a true likeness!

Here René Magritte has painted a self-portrait. Yet something isn't right this time either.
As if it were the most natural thing in the world he's cutting up his food with a knife and fork
and, at the same time, he's pouring a glass of wine while feeding himself some bread. Four
hands make light work!

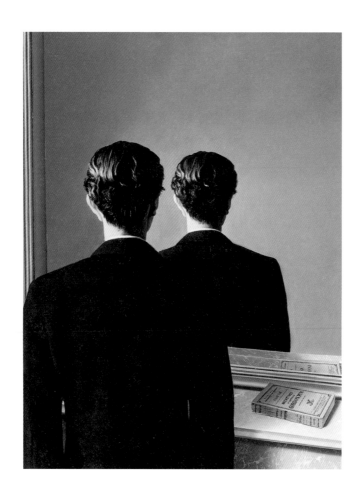

Two portraits...

Magritte seldom painted completely normal portraits. He found it boring when the model was immediately recognizable and there was nothing unusual to see in the picture. When friends or acquaintances asked him to paint their portrait he would think up surprising things.

Like with Edward James. He was an important person for Magritte since, as a rich art collector, he had bought several of his paintings. Magritte came up with a clever idea. He showed James from behind standing in front of

a mirror. Normally his face would be seen reflected in the mirror, as in the photograph of Magritte himself. But in this portrait it is different. In the mirror the back of his friend's head appears a second time, as you can see.

... or actually none at all?

Who is that then?
A flash of light like from a camera takes the place of the man's head.

Man Ray, a famous photographer who Magritte knew very well, photographed James several  times. This photo served as a model for this unusual portrait.

The Stone Age

Everything in this room has turned to stone as if an unseen hand has touched it with a magic wand. The man, the lion and the candle flame are frozen in a state of motionlessness. Soft things – the animal's fur, the man's coat, the tablecloth and the fruit in the bowl – have become as hard as stone. An eerie stillness spreads over the picture.

Can a stone be as light as a cloud?

"How can I paint a stone so that it is worth showing?" Magritte asked himself. When a completely normal stone floats like a cloud over the sea, it suddenly appears interesting and mysterious.

Who has ever heard of a water-nymph that, rather than having a fish's tail, has a fish's head instead? In any case, the mermaids we know from fairy-tales look completely different, don't they?

René Magritte painted his mermaid with the beautiful long legs of a woman and the large head and body of a fish. And, once again, our way of seeing things has been turned upside down. He often made use of such tricks by switching top and bottom, big and small, inside and outside, and alive and dead.

A topsy-turvy world

The front half of the shoes shown here are actually
the toes that are normally inside them! In these pictures nothing remains the way we usually imagine
things to be. We see the world with new eyes and are
made to think about things we would otherwise
never consider.

A topsy-turvy world

What is in front, and what is behind?

A woman is riding through the woods.

Most of the trees are behind her and the horse. That is why the tree trunk in the middle of the painting is hiding part of her body.

But wait, how can that be possible?

Immediately to the left of the woman there is a tree that is actually growing much further behind the one in the middle and yet it is hiding her arm and part of the stomach and left hindquarters of the horse.

To the right of the rider, the foreground and background have become completely confused. Her left hand and part of the horse vanish altogether, although this is actually a gap between two trees where we can look right into the background.

Curtains can be very mysterious because they hide something that not everyone should see. Curtains drawn across a window, for example, stop curious neighbours from looking in. A stage curtain in a theatre increases the tension before the performance begins.

The curtains in this picture though are mysterious just because they obviously do not conceal anything. They are alone on the beach in the dark, like actors on a stage. A narrow crescent moon bathes the strange scene in silvery light. The middle curtain is not made of any material at all. Although it is slightly in front of the two other curtains it seems like an opening through which a pale blue cloudy sky can be seen.

Peculiar Views

Astonishingly enough, this seagull doesn't have its usual plumage but rather a dress of clouds. At first it seems as if it is flying in the deep blue sky. Then again, the bird doesn't appear to have a solid body at all. Its outline seems like an opening in the night sky through which the bright of day can be seen. Magritte opens up the sky to show a second one beyond.

Here as well Magritte combines a night scene and a daylight sky at the same time in one picture. The sombre darkness of the night dominates the bottom half of the painting. Only a street lamp and the light in an upstairs room shine in the night and are reflected in the water in front of the house. The sky, on the other hand, is as bright as during the day. The dark outline of the trees stands out sharply against the clear blue sky and its soft white clouds.

Both day and night

Magritte painted several such pictures. He was very preoccupied with day and night. "This recall of day and night seems to me to have the power to surprise and enchant us", he once said in a television interview.

Mysterious relationships

One night, as Magritte recounted, an unusual thing happened to him. He woke up to find himself in a room with a birdcage, and inside the cage was a bird. Suddenly, instead of seeing the bird in the cage, there was a big egg, or so he thought. Somehow or other the cage and the egg appeared closely related in a most mysterious way. Many of Magritte's paintings show objects that, at first glance, do not seem to be related to each other in any way. He often spent a long time thinking about different objects which, when shown next to each other in one picture, would confront the viewer with an unfathomable mystery. In his opinion, each object only has one other object with which it could possibly be combined.

What do a steam train and a fireplace have in common? Everybody is familiar with a steam train. How could Magritte give it the magic of something out of the ordinary? The solution was to combine it with another equally well-known object, namely with a fireplace. That seemed much more unsettling and mysterious to him than if he had painted a Martian, an angel or a dragon next to the train. The real mystery can only be shown when using everyday things.

Do pictures actually show reality?

An easel stands in front of a window.
How peculiar that the painting on the canvas in front of the window
is an exact copy of the scenery which it is hiding!

But can we be certain?

Trees, bushes and meadows are both outside the room – as part of the
landscape – and inside the room, namely in the painting on the easel.
And it is exactly in this way, Magritte says, that we perceive the world. We
do not regard the world as part of ourselves. But, since we all have our
own idea as to what the world is like, this picture is, at the same time,
something that we always have within us.

In this painting the view out of the window was painted
on the window pane. Yet someone has smashed the glass.
Trees, field, sea and sky lie shattered on the floor, while the
hole in the window gives a view of the same scenery outside.
But what would we see if this scenery were also only a painting
and broke into little pieces?

The names of things

"This is not a pipe",

Magritte wrote in French on this picture. Of course it is a pipe – isn't it?

"Can you fill it?" Magritte asked an observer. "No, of course you can't

since it is only a picture. If I had written 'This is a pipe' under the

picture, I would have been lying!"

This is not a pipe, but only a *picture* of a pipe!

René Magritte felt that no object is really so

bound to its name that it could not be substituted for

another equally suitable word.

The cannon

A picture, however, can also replace a word in a sentence.

Magritte thought a great deal about the relationship between words, pictures, and objects. In this painting he gave the things new names.

the acacia   l'Acacia   la Lune   the moon

the snow   la Neige   le Plafond   the ceiling

the storm   l'Orage   le Désert   the desert

In just the same way as with these objects, the painter
invented unusual and surprising titles for his paintings. For
him, a picture was not finished without a title. He didn't want
to use words to explain his paintings but rather to intensify
their magic and mystery.

What do you think this picture could be called?

The titles of all the paintings in this book
are listed on page 28.

René Magritte was a painter whose mysterious pictures teach us to look at the world with new eyes. He led a completely normal life as an ordinary citizen, painting his pictures on an easel in the living room. He didn't like travelling, feeling most comfortable at home. Magritte died in 1967 at the age of 68, having spent most of his life in Brussels.

Today many people know him as the man with the black bowler hat. On the right you can see a picture he painted of such a man. And even here he couldn't help hiding the face. "Everything we see is hiding something else", Magritte said. And he meant that we always want to see what is hidden behind another object. This is his way of arousing our curiosity but we will never exactly know …

… who is hiding behind this apple?
Is it the painter himself, or one of his friends?

We will never completely solve the mysteries of René Magritte.

The Life of René Magritte

René Magritte was born on November 21, 1898 in the small Belgian town of Lessines. His brothers Raymond and Paul were two and four years younger than him. After leaving school René studied painting from 1916 to 1918 at the academy of art in Brussels. In June 1922 he married Georgette Berger. To earn money he worked as a pattern designer in a wallpaper factory, and later he designed advertising posters and exhibition booths for trade fairs. When he was 26 René sold his first painting. For a while, the Magrittes lived in Paris, then in 1930 returned to Brussels. René didn't like travelling, but, in 1937, he visited Edward James in London and, in 1965, he flew to the United States to his major exhibition at the Museum of Modern Art in New York. René Magritte died on August 15, 1967 in Brussels.